Echo Dot 3rd Generation User Guide

The Complete Amazon Echo 3rd Generation Instruction Manual with Alexa for Beginners

Paul O. Garten

....

This book comes with a **FREE** eBook titled:
"Mastering Alexa in One Day with Over 620 Voice Commands."
It's big. It's powerful. It's rich. Don't miss it.
See download link on the last page.

....

Echo Dot 3rd Generation User Guide

The Complete Amazon Echo 3rd Generation Instruction Manual with Alexa for Beginners

Contents

Introduction

Alexa, with your Echo speaker can wake you from sleep; go shopping for you or keep you company with folktales. She's such a wonderful friend and personal assistant. Activated with the voice, the Echo Dot 3rd generation can process and deliver on specific actions for thousands of Alexa voice commands. It can control smart home devices, make and receive calls, stream music from connected music platforms, and so much more.

Over the years, Amazon has continued on a journey to revolutionize the technology world and they are particularly leading the control of smart home devices. The Amazon Echo Dot 3rd generation is an improvement on the 2nd generation Echo Dot and can fit for your living or bedroom.

It can be effortless, enjoyable and rewarding to use the Amazon Echo Dot if you can converse perfectly with Alexa. The steps to getting the best from your Echo speaker are fully explained in this book. You will learn so much about how to make the most of your Amazon Echo Dot 3rd generation smart device. The book offer detailed explanations on topics such as; settings and customizations of the Amazon Echo Dot, meaning of visual indicators on the Echo Dot, teaching Alexa to always recognize your voice, setting a household profile, setting up music services, deleting your voice recordings, multi-room music setup with the Amazon Echo Dot, how to create customize skills for Alexa, building and creating a group for your smart home devices, shopping Amazon securely with Alexa, IFTTT integration with Alexa and so much more. As you continue using the product, keep your eyes open to more possibilities that it can help you accomplish. With IFTTT, many auto functions can be triggered.

Finally, this book details how to set up your Echo Dot, settings, commands, tips and tricks on how you can get the best of what your Echo device and Amazon Alexa has to offer. It is completely a simplified guide to help you master your Amazon Echo Dot.

Chapter 1

Getting Started

Unboxing

The package comes with a power adapter (15W), a quick start guide and the Echo Dot 3rd generation smart device. By default, the device registers to your Amazon account, hence, check the **gift option** if this is a gift for someone (just below the Buy Now button) when buying it on Amazon.

Amazing features of the Amazon Echo Dot 3rd Generation over its 2nd Generation

The Amazon Echo Dot 3rd generation is an improvement on its previous models with amazing features.

(1) It has a fabric design and can easily blend with the decoration of your room.

(2) It is easy to set up and integrate with other smart devices.

(3) It has a clear call quality.

(4) Audio quality is louder, clearer and refined than former models.

(5) It has Bluetooth and 3.5mm audio outputs.

(6) It can be activated with a voice.

(7) It can easily be hooked to a Bluetooth speaker or stereo for better sound production using an AUX cable or through Bluetooth. Sadly, the package doesn't come with a 3.5mm AUX audio jack. You'll have to buy one.

(8) A little bigger than the 2nd generation model.

(9) It uses 4 powerful far-field microphones and can pick up your voice from any corner of your room.

(10) It responds quicker than previous models.

(11) A larger speaker than previous models.

Technical Details

Size: 3.9" W x 3.9" H x 1.7" Base depth.

Weight: 10.6 oz (300 g).

Wi-Fi: 802.11 a/b/g/n (2.4 & 5 GHz) protocol. Can't connect to a peer-to-peer WiFi network.

Processor: Intel Atom.

Audio: Built-in speaker with 3.5 mm audio output.

Bluetooth: A2DP Protocol; can't connect to Bluetooth speakers that ask for PIN codes.

Warranty: 90 days.

Echo Dot vs Echo vs Echo Plus

Similarities

[1] All the Echo devices can conveniently exercise control over smart home devices.

[2] All the Echo devices can stream music.

[3] All Echos have Bluetooth.

[4] All can make free calls (audio only) to US, Canada and Mexico.

[5] There's presence of line-out with 3.5mm audio cable in all the Echos.

Differences

[1] **Speaker:** 1.6 inches for Echo Dot; 2.5 inches woofer 0.6 inches tweeter for Echo and 3 inches woofer and 0.8 inches tweeter for Echo Plus.

[2] While the Amazon Echo and Echo Plus have dual speakers with Dolby Processing, the Echo Dot lacks these features.

[3] Only the Echo Plus has Zigbee hub built in it.

[4] There's presence of line-in in Echo Plus. This feature is lacking in Echo Dot and Echo.

Setting up the Echo Dot in Your Home

Setting up the Echo Dot is pretty straightforward. It's up to you to decide where you want to place your Echo device but make sure you don't place it too close to the window or walls.

Connect to a Source of Power Supply

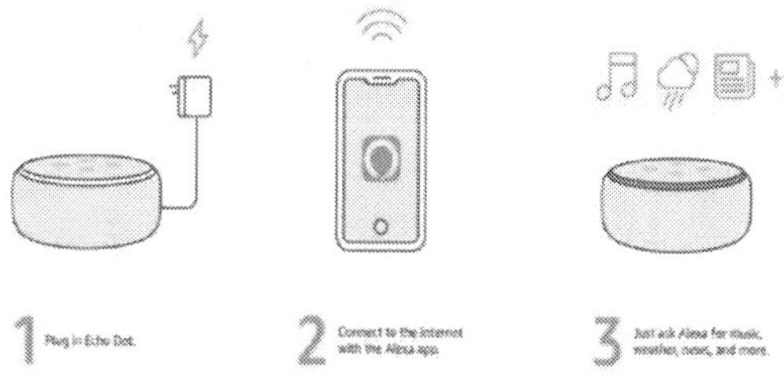

The set up begins with putting it on, i.e., connecting it to a power outlet (mains) with the power adapter that came with it. Once done, the Echo Dot begins to respond to the power supplied to it.

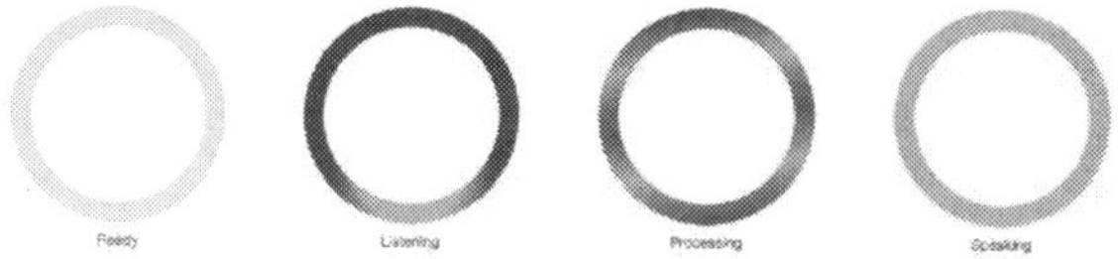

Moments later, the ring color changes to orange (connecting) and then you are greeted by Alexa telling you that your device is ready for setup. Again, make sure you keep it 10 inches or more away from the walls or obstructions.

Download the Alexa App and Connect to a WiFi Network

Now, press the action button, and for the first time doing this, Alexa would tell you that your device is not registered. Proceed with the registration of your device. Depending on your device's mobile operating system (Fire (3.0 or higher), Android (5.0 or higher) or iOS (9.0 or higher)), visit the App Store (Amazon or Apple) or Play Store, search for and download the Amazon Alexa app and have it installed on your phone.

To activate Alexa when installation is complete, launch the application and enter your existing Amazon account details. **Sign In** to continue. Where you don't have an existing Amazon account, **Tap Create A New Amazon Account** to sign up with Amazon and then sign into the app with your new account details.

Once signed in, **Get Started** with the Alexa application. Select your name and **Help Alexa Get to Know You.** If your name isn't showed, tap **I'm Someone Else.** Done with that? Then begin to customize your app. You may choose to use a nickname, full name or just anything for calling and messaging; you may still be required to enter your full name. **Continue** when done. Tap **Allow** to permit Amazon Alexa to upload your contacts on from your phone so that you can connect with others. You can always do this later if you are not comfortable doing it immediately. In this case, simply tap **Later**.

Connect and verify your mobile phone number to enable your Alexa calling and messaging feature between you and others who has this number via Alexa. Amazon would send a 6-digit verification code to the phone number you inputted, insert the code on your app and **Continue** to finish the setup. You can as well **Skip** and do this later.

From here, you can begin to customize (this would be covered in subsequent chapters) the Alexa app. To start requesting from Alexa immediately without your Echo device, tap on the Alexa icon on the homepage. Grant her permission to use the phone's microphone and you are **Done**. Every time you need her, tap on the Alexa icon then make your request.

We can now identify what is what on the Alexa home page.

You can also visit http://alexa.amazon.com from your PC or mobile browser for Alexa on the web. Open and sign in to your Amazon Alexa using your login credentials. Take note that the Alexa app does not work with the first and second Kindle Fire Generations.

In connecting the Echo Dot to the Internet, it is highly recommended that you use a WiFi. A mobile hotspot should be your last resort. To begin, launch the Alexa app, tap the **Menu**  icon and from **Settings**, choose your Echo device and **Update WiFi**. Next, **Select a new device**. On the Echo Dot, press and hold the **Action** button for 5 seconds. Once the light turns **orange**, a list of available WiFi networks is displayed on your mobile phone. Select your preferred network. Enter required WiFi login password if needed. You can manually add your WiFi network if it is not listed, scroll down and **Add a Network. Rescan** and **Connect** again if you can't still connect to a WiFi. Viola, Alexa is ready!

Understanding light ring status

The light ring communicates the mode of your Echo Dot to you.

[1] The device is on standby mode and awaits your request when all lights go off.

[2] The Echo Dot is starting up when a solid blue light shows with a spinning cyan light as shown below.

[3] The device processes your request when a solid blue color shows while a cyan color stays and point to the direction of someone speaking to Alexa as shown below.

[4] When a solid blue color alternates with cyan, the Echo Dot is responding to a request.

[5] A spinning orange color light in a clockwise direction shows that the Echo Dot is connecting to the internet through your WiFi network as depicted below.

[6] When the microphones are turned off, the Echo device shows a solid red light. You can always turn on the microphones by pressing the **Microphone** button. See the illustration below.

[7] A pulsing yellow color light shows that you have a message or notification. You can access them by saying, "Alexa, what messages do I have?" or "Alexa, what notifications do I have?"

[8] A pulsing green color light shows a Drop In action, or it means you are receiving a call.
[9] When a green color light spins clockwise, it means the Echo Dot is making a call, or you are Dropping In on another person's device.

[10] Volume adjustment action shows a white light on the device.

[11] During WiFi setup, a continuous pulsing violet color light shows that an error has occurred. Repeat the process.

[12] A purple flash light after interacting with Alexa shows that the Do Not Disturb feature is enabled.

Things to Try Immediately with your Echo Dot

Get started with Alexa right now without having to go through much detail.

Getting Started

"Alexa, are you okay?"

"Alexa, good night."

"Alexa, tell me some joke."

"Alexa, sing a song for me."

"Alexa, can we play a game?"

"Alexa, what happened this day in history?"

"Alexa, can you recommend where to buy an ice cream?"

"Alexa, play latest Amazon Music."

“Alexa, find out some free books on Audible?”

“Alexa, define Physics?”

“Alexa, translate ‘happy birthday’ to French?”

“Alexa, let’s go shopping”

“Alexa, what do I have on my calendar today?”

“Alexa, set a countdown timer for 30 minutes.”

"Alexa, what can I prepare for dinner?"

"Alexa, add a reminder about going to a meeting by 1:00 PM on Thursday."

"Alexa, convert $200 US dollars to Euros."

"Alexa, tell me about the weather in Paris."

Basic Sound Controls

“Alexa, volume up.”

“Alexa, lower.”

“Alexa, turn up the volume.”

“Alexa, volume 5.”

Time & Date

“Alexa, what’s the time”
“Alexa, what's today’s date?”
“Alexa, when is my next alarm?”
“Alexa, cancel my alarm for 4 p.m.”
“Alexa, snooze”

"Alexa, when is [holiday name / notable date] this year?"

Wake Word, User profiles and Accounts

"Alexa, how can I change the wake word?"

"Alexa, can all my Echo devices bear the same name?"

"Alexa, switch accounts."

"Alexa, which user profile is this?"

Bluetooth and WiFi

"Alexa, pair."

"Alexa, Bluetooth."

"Alexa, link up my phone."

"Alexa, can I pair up my smartphone with you?"

"Alexa, connect to the WiFi?"

Books:
Audiobooks

"Alexa, read my audiobooks."

"Alexa, find free books on Audible."

"Alexa, read Educated from Audible."

"Alexa, stop reading in 20 minutes."

"Alexa, sign up for Audible."

"Alexa, what's popular on Audible this week?"

Kindle Books

"Alexa, read my eBooks."

"Alexa, read Becoming from Kindle."

Playback controls:

"Alexa, next chapter."

"Alexa, pause."

"Alexa, previous chapter."

"Alexa, jump ahead."

"Alexa, restart the book."

"Alexa, stop reading in 10 minutes."

"Alexa, restart the chapter."

"Alexa, resume."

Communication Basic controls:

"Alexa, answer."

"Alexa, hang up."

"Alexa, turn on 'Do-Not-Disturb.'"

Calling and Messaging

"Alexa, call Allen."

"Alexa, call Mom's mobile."

"Alexa, message Paul."

"Alexa, read my messages."

Drop In

"Alexa, drop in."

"Alexa, drop in on Computer."

Announcements

"Alexa, announce that we have to leave now."

"Alexa, broadcast that everyone should come for dinner."

"Alexa, announce that I am on my home."

Donations

"Alexa, donate."

"Alexa, donate $200 to Doctors Without Borders."

Fun with Alexa

Songs:

"Alexa, sing me a song."

"Alexa, sing a worship song."

"Alexa, sing a winter song."

"Alexa, sing a love song."

"Alexa, rap for me."

"Alexa, sing for me the national anthem of the USA."

"Alexa, sing a song of the 80s."

"Alexa, sing RnB song."

"Alexa, sing for my baby."

"Alexa, sing for my grandma."

"Alexa, sing a hymn."

"Alexa, sing 'Great is Thy Faithfulness.'"

Chapter 2

Settings & Customization

Waking the Echo Dot

Call her by her default name—Alexa and she will respond. The blue color LED light on the Echo Dot indicates that Alexa is listening to your command. You can begin to try some commands like: “Alexa, how are you,” or “Alexa, what’s the weather today?”

Changing the Wake Word

The Amazon Echo device's default wake word is set to "Alexa." Once you call that, Alexa is alerted and waiting for next command. Just maybe you have another Echo device bearing the name, “Alexa,” you may want to give another name to your new Dot since if leaving the two to bear Alexa would create confusion. You can change it to something else, e.g., Amazon, Echo or Computer. On the Alexa app homepage, tap on **Devices**  and select the Echo device you want to rename. Go to **Wake Word**. Choose **Amazon, Computer** or **Echo** from the list and **Save**. Take note that the system would have to be updated for the new wake word to take effect and during this time, your Amazon Alexa smart device can't work.

On the other hand, you can initiate the process by saying, "Alexa, change my wake word."

Changing your Echo and other Smart Home devices' name

By default, your device is configured with your first and product name, e.g., Garten's Echo Dot. Go ahead and change to a preferred name via **Settings** and **Save** when done. You can choose to change it to represent where it's being used, e.g., bedroom Echo Dot. This works best if you have more than one Echo device in your home.

To rename your smart home devices, tap the **Menu** icon and select **Smart Home**. From the list, tap on the smart device you want to rename and then the **ellipses** icon and **Edit Name.** Hit **Done** to save your new device name. However, take note that you are only renaming the device for Alexa only. It is advisable that you also rename the device from its companion app (if any).

To disable a device
Toggle the **Enabled** button under it to **Disabled**.

Setting your location

Some services largely depend on knowing your location to deliver on location-specific requests, e.g., weather and traffic information. Set your ZIP, street address, etc. in the location settings.

To change your location in the Alexa app, tap the **Devices**  icon on the homepage, select your Echo device and tap **Device Location**. Type in your address and **Save**.

Note: If more than one Echo device is connected to your account, you'll have to update their location one after the other.

Sound Settings

Your Echo Dot's alarm seems too quiet? You can fix that. In the Alexa app, tap **Devices** from the home page and select your **Echo Dot**. To change the default sound, navigate to **Sounds & Notifications.** You can as well set Alexa to play a sound while listening to your command and another when done processing the command. This is particularly necessary if you have your Echo device placed out of sight where it isn't possible to see the LED ring light responding to commands.

The Do-Not-Disturb feature

The do-not-disturb feature can turn Alexa off at a certain or scheduled time of the day to prevent calls, messages and drop-ins with exception of alarms and timers. However, this can only be set once per day and same time for other days of the week till you schedule a new time. To set a Do-Not-Disturb, tap on the **Devices** icon in the Alexa mobile app and choose your device then enable Do-Not-Disturb by **toggling** it on [so that the dot rest by right] and also create your **Schedule** for it. Tap on **Start** to set start time and **End** to set end time.

Setting up Echo Dot in different locations within the house

Setting up different Echo Dot in different locations follows the same method like setting up the device for the first time but this time choosing a different name for your new Echo Dot. Again, you don't necessarily need to start tuning other settings. It'll pick up automatically.

Setting Alexa on Whisper Mode

As the name suggests, the Whisper Mode enables you to whisper to Alexa while she whispers back to you so that none of you disturbs other members of the family should they were sleeping. To turn on / off whisper mode, simply say, "Alexa, turn [on/off] whisper mode.”

Deleting voice recordings from Alexa history

Sometimes the Amazon Echo triggers inadvertently and starts recording sounds within its reach considering her sharp microphones. You may not know that you have recordings in Alexa history. This may not really be a factor but if you feel the device must have recorded sensitive information then it becomes something to worry about.

To be on the safe side, you can choose to clear your Alexa history. To get started, go to **Settings** on your Alexa app and tap on **Alexa Account** then **History**. At **History**, you can see all your saved recordings. Go ahead and delete them one after the other. However, to delete everything at once, from your PC, log in to your Amazon account and go to **Content & Devices**. Click on **Your Devices** and select the **Alexa device** you want to erase all recordings then **Manage Voice Recordings**, choose the option to erase everything.

Chapter 3

Building A Smart Home And Linking Your Devices To Alexa

Building a smart home is about binding your smart devices with the Amazon Alexa so that she can control them any time you request her to do so. Devices can be connected to Alexa and controlled individually or as a group using a single voice command by creating a smart home group.

Apart from your Amazon Echo devices, you can also connect your other smart devices to Alexa and have her control them when you request her to do so using your voice. Note that for a seamless communication between your Alexa-enabled smart home devices with the Alexa mobile app, it is highly recommended that you connect all these devices using the same WiFi network.

Again, when making an order for a smart device with intention of pairing same to Amazon Alexa, make sure that such a device is certified by Amazon to be compatible with Alexa. Follow the link here to browse through Amazon recommendations in this regard:

https://www.amazon.com/b?node=6563140011.

Linking your Bluetooth Speaker / Home Stereo System with your Echo Dot

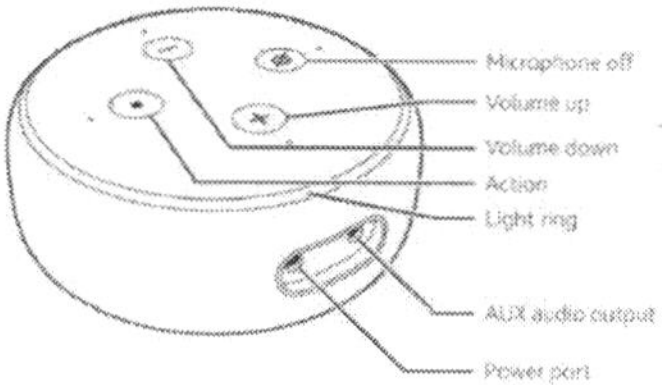

Pairing your Bluetooth speaker means that you have connected your Echo device to Alexa before this time and hence linking a Bluetooth speaker to the Echo device. Linking a smart speaker to your Echo device is especially important if you want to improve the sound quality of your Echo speaker and hence, connecting an external speaker to it via Bluetooth or using an audio cable.

To pair a Bluetooth speaker, keep the speaker 3—5 feet away from your Echo Dot and tune it to be on pairing mode. Next, go to the Alexa mobile app and tap **Menu**,  from **Settings**, select your Echo Dot, and then **Bluetooth**. Allow scanning to be completed then choose your Bluetooth speaker and finally, you are done setting up your speaker.

To connect your Echo Dot to your Home Stereo System, use a 3.5mm audio output to connect the two together. You can also connect your wired headphone to your Echo device by plugging in the 3.5mm headphone input to the AUX audio output of your Echo Dot (see the audio jack behind the device).

Linking your Mobile Device to your Echo Device

You can stream music services from your phone and have them playing on your Echo speaker. To begin, get to **Settings** on your smartphone then **Bluetooth**. Toggle your Bluetooth on, and shortly, you would find your Echo device under **Available devices**. Give Alexa a command to pair your smartphone, e.g., “Alexa, pair,” while you tap on your Echo device. You can choose to cancel the pairing while it’s still going on (“Alexa, cancel”) or disconnect your smartphone from your Echo device (“Alexa, disconnect”). To connect again in the future, you can simply say, “Alexa, connect,” and Alexa would pair up to the same or last Bluetooth device paired with it.

Linking other Smart Home Devices to Alexa

Two methods suffice to linking other smart home devices to Alexa.

Linking your devices to Alexa using Guided Discovery

To link a smart home device that is not ZigBee-supported but WiFi enabled, power the device and launch the Alexa mobile application and from the home page, tap **Devices** 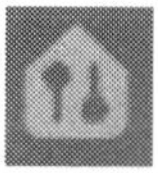 then the **plus**  icon, and finally **Add Device**. Select your smart home device as well as the brand of the device. Follow the onscreen guide to complete the process.

Linking your devices to Alexa using Smart Home Skills

A third-party skill or a companion application for your device serves as the enabler for the smart device with Alexa. In other words, when enabled, you can easily link your smart device that associates with it with Alexa. Every smart device, especially those not manufactured by Amazon, comes with an enabler app otherwise referred to as skill.

To link up your device with Alexa using a skill, power on the smart device and in the Alexa app, go to **Menu** then **Skills**. Touch the search icon and type the skill name for your device then conduct a search for it. From the search result, tap the skill for your device and **Enable** it. Follow the instruction shown on the screen to complete the process which involves connecting your smart device to Alexa.

Take note that once your smart home device is set up with the Amazon Alexa using the required skill for the device, anyone with the right command can trigger the smart device to work. Hence, it is recommended that you put off the microphones on your Echo device when leaving the house as well as setting up a PIN code on your smartphone that holds the Alexa app to prevent authorized access to Alexa through your mobile phone.

How to create a Smart Home Group

A smart home group enables all devices that are members of the group to be controlled using a single command at a time.

To create a smart home group in the Alexa app, go to **Menu**, **Devices** and then tap the **Plus**  icon. Finally, tap on **Add Group**. Enter your preferred or select from the suggested names. Tap **Next** and select your smart devices for the group and **Save**. You can come back later to take out or add more items to the group.

From here, you can say, "Alexa, turn on {group 1}," or "Alexa, play Celine Dion on {group 2}" where group 1 may be 3 smart security light bulbs, and group 2 may be 3 Echo speakers spread across rooms. However, take note that your Echo device can only be connected to one smart home group at one time.

Another way to set up a smart group in the Alexa app is by going to **Menu** 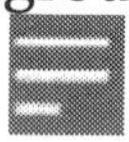 , then **Smart Home** but have in mind that this feature support only smart devices that work by switching, e.g., light bulbs, plugs, etc. Tap the **Groups** tab then **Add Group**. Pick a name for your smart home group from the list or enter a custom name. Next, **define your group** by adding an Echo speaker considering your selection/location in the previous screen. The Echo speaker is to enable you to control the smart home devices you'd be adding to the group within the location of the Echo speaker. Once you've added an Echo speaker to the group, go ahead and select the devices you'd like to add to the group within the location of the Echo speaker. When done, tap **Save**. You can still add or remove an item from the list later. Can't find your smart devices listed? Then go back and enable the skill associated with that smart device from the Skill store (*see* Menu => Skills & Games) then tell Alexa to discover your device ("Alexa, discover my devices").

Now, if you go back to check under the **Group**'s page in Smart Home, you'd find your newly created group sitting there. Within the Group tab, groups with an Echo speaker in them are marked Alexa-enabled. Tap the group name to see its ON/OFF switch buttons.

How to edit a Smart Home Group

You can always add or remove members to/from a smart home group after creating it. To get started, go to **Menu, Smart Home** and tap the **Group** tab. From the displayed groups, select a group and **Edit Name**. Remove any existing member of the group or add more members to the group. You can **Trash** the group from here.

IFTTT with Alexa

Make your life easy by automating certain things that you are supposed to be doing manually. You don't need watching over or doing things that can easily be automated. With the IFTTT protocol, your life can become a bit easier and less disordered. IFTTT is an acronym for If This Then That. This means that if a specific condition is met, then a certain action should be triggered. Whether you call it IFTTT applets or recipes, they all mean the same thing and are designed to trigger your IFTTT controlled devices and make your life interesting. All that is needed is for you to set them up and enjoy all it has to offer.

Fortunately and unfortunately, IFTTT recipes work more with Android OS. In this section, I'll try to show you how you can use IFTTT to automate your home with few examples. To get started with IFTTT, visit http://ifttt.com, sign up or sign in. From the Channels home, click on Amazon Alexa and enter your Amazon login details. Scroll and check out existing Recipes for Alexa. You can also download the IFTTT mobile app from Playstore or Appstore for Android OS and iOS respectively.

Below are few IFTTT recipes to demonstrate how it works and how you can move on from here with IFTTT.

To keep a record of songs that you play

You can decide to keep a record of songs you've listened to on Alexa. This recipe adds the name of the song, name of the artiste, album name, etc. to a Google spreadsheet in Google Drive. Sadly, this IFTTT cannot add songs from sample clips, podcast or even Pandora. Once you locate the applet, click on Add/Turn On then permit IFTTT to access Alexa and authorize IFTTT in Alexa and finally Authorize IFTTT in Google Docs and click on Save.

Remove your phone from silence

Are you trying to find a phone you put on silent and misplaced? Alexa can help you with an IFTTT applet to remove your phone from silence. Browse for and turn on this applet then set a keyword you'll love to use in triggering it. Default keyword is "Alexa, trigger unsilence phone." You can set any new keyword that you find comfortable. Example, "Alexa, trigger find my phone." Once initiated, your Android phone's volume would be tune to 100% and removed from silent. From here, you can tell Alexa to call your phone.

IFTTT to call your phone

You can have Alexa call your phone by saying, "Alexa, trigger find my phone." Like any other, search and select the recipe then Add/Turn it on and grant it needed permissions. Set preferred keyword or leave it at default and save. This recipe may be location dependent.

To change the color of your Philips Hue bulb

You can simply browse or search the IFTTT recipe database with the keyword, “Tell Alexa to change the color of your Hue bulb” to add this applet to your Alexa. Before this time, your Philips Hue bulb must have been paired with your Echo Dot. Grant needed permission and save settings. You can then tell Alexa, “Alexa, trigger blue bedroom light” and see what happen. You can also trigger other light colors, e.g., yellow, white, red, etc. Refer to color Hex codes for more color options.

Alexa can also trigger party mood in your home with Philips Hue bulb

Browse for and add/turn on “Tell Alexa to start the party and put your lights on color loop.” Grant IFTTT and Save. The voice command is “Alexa, trigger party time.”

This is just a few examples to show what IFTTT can do for you. Follow same method to set up other IFTTT recipes that you may want to use. But remember to pair corresponding hardware to your Echo Dot before searching and turning on the needed IFTTT applet to power them.

Here are some Smart Home commands depending on corresponding smart devices to work with them.

Smart Home Invocation Phrases

Lights

To turn on/off your light: "Alexa, turn the security lights [on / off]."

To control light intensity: "Alexa, [dim / brighten] {light location or light group name}."

Plugs

General format: "Alexa, turn on / off {plug name}."

Thermostat

To check the Thermostat: "Alexa, what's the temperature of the Thermostat?" "Alexa, set the thermostat to <#> degrees" or "Alexa, reduce the temperature of the Thermostat."

Door lock

To lock the door: "Alexa, lock the [front / back] door."

To unlock: "Alexa, unlock the door."

To check your doors: "Alexa, is the [front / back] door locked?"

Cameras

You can get live feeds from your cameras mounted within your house using the Alexa app, Echo Spot, Echo Show or Fire TV smart device.

To get feeds from any of your camera: "Alexa, show me the [front / back] door."

Microwave

"Alexa, set the microwave for <#> minutes."

Fan

To speed up or slow your fan speed,
"Alexa, set fan speed in {fan location name} to {#} percent"

Notes:
(a) Set up a code for unlocking your doors when enabling "Unlock by Voice" Alexa skill for your doors.

(b) Invocation phrases are set by smart device manufacturers. Thus, phrases use here might vary slightly.

Chapter 4

Amazon Profiling

Setting Your User Profile—Teaching Alexa to always recognize Your Voice

Voice training can be done by setting up a Voice or User Profile. The essence of doing this is to enable Alexa understands you better and interact with you closely—as you! You can refer to this as customized interactions. This feature is available on the Amazon Echo, Echo Plus, Echo Dot, Spot and Echo Show.

To get started, launch the Alexa app, tap the **Menu**  icon and go to **Settings, Accounts** and finally tap on **Your Voice**. **Begin** the process of making Alexa learn your voice. You can also initiate this process with a voice command: "Alexa, [learn / train] my voice."

If using the mobile app to create a voice profile, tapping the **drop-down** menu would show devices that you have. Select a device and start the process. Right now, it is important that you turn off the microphones ("Alexa, turn off microphones on {Echo dot device name}") of other Echo devices in the house (if any) while you concentrate with the selected one. Since this process is conducted using the Alexa app, you may not necessarily need to repeat it with other Echo devices you might have in your house. They'll automatically pick up.

Once the process is initiated, Alexa would lead you through the training with voice prompts. Say them out loud with your natural voice, and from a position you may sit or stand to send requests. Don't go too close to your Echo device. Again, try to reduce background noise as much as possible and keep your Echo device away from walls (say 10 inches away). If you miss a prompt and Alexa doesn't get it right, **Try Again. Complete** the process when you get to the end.

At this point, you can connect your voice profile to your **Amazon Music Unlimited** account. Continue to use the device when the process is completed and try to check if Alexa can recognize your voice after 30 minutes by asking her who you are.

If you have any issue, reach out to Amazon via Help & Feedback. Select the concerned device and log your complaint.

To create more voice profiles with the same Echo, new users must download the Alexa app into their mobile phones and sign in to the Amazon account that hosts the Echo device and then initiate the process from their Alexa mobile app. Again, the essence of this is to have a personalized experience with Alexa such as news briefings, making calls and messaging from contact lists, etc.

From time to time, ask Alexa who you are before making request to be sure she's listening and processing commands from the right person. If she's wrong on who's talking, tell her to stop or cancel so that you don't access another person's content. As you keep using Alexa, it masters your voice even more.

How to Delete a Voice Profile

In the Alexa app, go to Settings => Alexa Account => Recognized Voices => Your Voice => Delete my Voice. Note that deleting a Voice Profile means that you'll no longer enjoy a personalized experience with Alexa.

Setting a Household Profile

A Household Profile enables you to share contents (e.g., audiobooks, calendars, music, etc.), manage account features (e.g., to-do lists, shopping list, etc.) and access customized content (e.g., traffic, news). The Amazon Household Profile settings permit 2 adults Amazon accounts and up to 4 child accounts. While adult accounts can be added directly through the app, the child accounts can only be added through **FreeTime**.

To create a Household Profile, open your Alexa app, select Menu and go to Settings => Alexa Account => Amazon Household. Begin the process by tapping **Start** to add a household member. Alexa prompt you to **Pass Your Device** to the person that would like to join your household so that they can sign in to their account. If they are not available, you can get their username and password to complete the process on their behalf then have them **Join Household** and finally, the **Household Is Created.**

The new person added needs to complete the process by logging into the Alexa app. You can sign out and allow them sign in with their details using your device to complete the process.

Adding a Child Account would require you go through FreeTime. In the Alexa app and from **Menu** , go to **Settings**, and tap on the Echo device meant for this to get started. Find **FreeTime** under **General**. In **FreeTime Settings**, toggle it to **Enable**. **Setup Amazon FreeTime** by Enabling desired features just by toggling them and **Continue** when done.

Manage your Child's Profile at **Parent's Dashboard** using the link: **Take Me to Parent's Dashboard**. At Parent's Dashboard, you can monitor your child's activities and adjust what features the child can access.

To switch between accounts, say, "Alexa, switch {account name} account." The new person takes charge of Alexa. While this works only for adult account; to switch to a child's account, the FreeTime feature must be turned ON, and OFF when going back to an adult account. See FreeTime Settings to Enable or Disable it. Once FreeTime is turned OFF, the account switches to previous adult that used the device. You can always find out whose account you are using by saying, "Alexa, whose account is this?"

Important Notice:
[1] A second adult added to your Amazon Household can actually use your payment method to buy from Amazon and also view your Prime Photos.

[2] Since you'll be possibly sharing your Amazon profile, it is advisable that you create a Confirmation Code for your voice purchases.

To switch between profiles, just say, "Alexa, switch accounts."

To check user profile, ask, “Alexa, which account am I using?”

How to Delete a Household Profile

Go to Amazon Household in the Alexa mobile app and select **Remove** against the user’s profile. If it’s you, tap **Leave**.

Chapter 5

What Alexa Skills Do You Need For Your Device?

Alexa Skills are 3rd party applications that work with Alexa. They help binds smart home devices to Alexa and also serve as utility apps or games. Nowadays, apart from Amazon developers, anyone can come up with an idea of how they want Alexa to respond to them when they send a command and turn that into a skill for Alexa. See how you can create your custom skills in the section, "Alexa Blueprints—How to Create Custom Skills for Amazon Alexa."

How to Access and Enable Alexa Skills

You can access thousands of Alexa Skills through the web. Visit http://alexa.amazon.com using your computer and log in with your Amazon login details. Browse through the categories and Enable any skill that you like.

You can also access Alexa Skills from your Alexa app. To get started, open the Alexa mobile app, tap **Menu** then **Skills &**

Games. Browse through **Featured** or **All Categories** to see skills you can enable. Once you find your desired skill, tap on it and Enable it.

To enable Alexa Skill with your voice, use the format: "Alexa, enable {skill name}," e.g., "Alexa, enable Jeopardy." This works best when you know a skill name but where you don't, you would have to browse through the categories in the Alexa app.

Skills are particularly important in binding your smart home device to Alexa. Where necessary, download, install, and setup a companion that comes with the device then search and **Enable** associated skill for the smart device in the Alexa application. Once the skill for the device is enabled and the device is powered on, tell Alexa to discover it by saying: "Alexa, discover devices."

To see all the skills you've enabled in your Amazon Alexa account, in the Alexa app, go to your **Skills & Games** page from the **Menu**

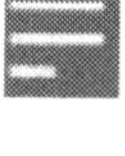

then tap **Your Skills**.

How to Disable a Skill

Following from the above, you can disable any skill you want from the **Your Skills** tab. Tap on the skill then **Disable** it. Alternatively, using your voice, you can say, "Alexa, disable {skill name}" and the skill would be disabled.

Alexa Blueprint—How to Create Custom Skills for Amazon Alexa

Apart from Amazon developers, even you right now can begin to develop Alexa skills using your ideas and have those skills work for you just the way you want when you send a voice command to Alexa.

To start creating skills right now, visit https://blueprints.amazon.com with your computer and login with your Amazon login details. Supply required information then pick a template or blueprint to start creating your custom skill. You can create a quiz game, fairy tale, etc. Go through the Featured Blueprints to see what's available. You can also go through the Blueprints categories.

As soon as you find a template that you would like to work with, click on it to see more details on how to create something out of it. Customizing a blueprint is straightforward. Listen to the sample of the Blueprint and **Make Your Own.** Give your Blueprint a simple straight name. You can always come back to edit the **Skills You've Made** by clicking on the **Edit** button for your skill. See option at the top of the Blueprint homepage.

Give minutes for your Skill to be ready. The system notifies when your skill is ready. Look out for a green notification message. Once **Ready to Use,** you can enable the skill for your device. For example, "Alexa, open Quizzer," where 'Quizzer' is your custom skill name.

At any time, you can disable or delete a skill from your account via **Skills You've Made** if you aren't comfortable with it.

How to Find Best Alexa Skills

There are thousands of skills on Amazon. This makes it hard to find great skills to enable.

Few steps can help you find great skills:

(a) Visit Amazon Alexa skills page using a PC: https://www.amazon.com/alexa-skills/b?ie=UTF8&node=13727921011.

(b) See Alexa skills categories by left.

(c) For example, click Movies & TV and Sort by Avg. Customer Review.

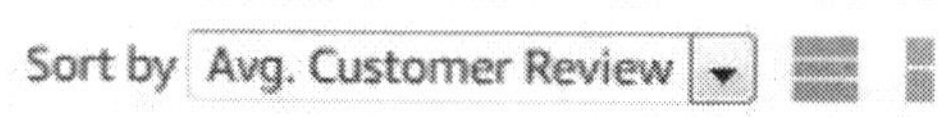

(d) The sorted result seems to be great based on Customer Reviews. Once you find a skill that you love, click on it to open then Enable it on the page.

Chapter 6

Alexa Routine

When set up is done, Alexa can perform multiple actions with just a single voice command. For example, you can say, “Alexa, I’m stepping out” to have her switch the lights and plugs off, or maybe saying, “Alexa, what’s in the news” to have her play your flash briefings.

Alexa Routines with the Amazon Echo Devices

Alexa routines can automate how your Echo device works with other Smart Home Devices. A command is sent to Alexa and that follows your Smart Device being triggered for action. For example, you can set "Alexa, good night" to turn off your smart light bulbs. Alexa routines can work a range of Amazon Echo including but not limited to Amazon Echo, Echo Plus, Echo Show, and Echo Dot.

Alexa routines can stop audio or play it for minutes, make announcements, send notifications or trigger a Do-Not-Disturb for a time.

How to Create a Common Amazon Alexa Routine

To get started with Alexa routine, launch the Alexa app, tap on the **Menu** 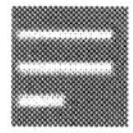 then select **Routines** and create a routine using the plus  icon at the top right side of the screen. Create a trigger via **When This Happen**. Now, you can either create a routine when you **Say A Phrase** (first option) or at **Scheduled Time** (second option).

Creating a Routine with a Phrase

If selecting the first option, enter a phrase, e.g., "Alexa, how is traffic now?" and tap on **Done**. Next, add an action to work with the phrase you just set via **Add** action. Here, there are actions such as news, traffic, smart home or weather. For instance, if you select Traffic [and Done], Alexa will then give you traffic information when called upon for your default location with the phrase, "Alexa, how is traffic now?" and that automatically becomes a routine anytime you command Alexa with that phrase. This is just an example.

Creating a Routine at Scheduled Time and Day

If going for the second option, choose the time you would like your routine to be activated and also choose when you want it to repeat. Here, you can decide to choose once a week, or every day, etc. Confirm your selection and tap **Done**. Next, add an action against the time and day(s) you want your routine to occur by tapping on the plus icon. Such an action can be getting weather information, news, playing music, traffic, triggering a smart home device, etc. and you are **Done**.

Adding Smart Home Devices to Routine

To make this even more beautiful with a Smart Home Device, on the previous screen, instead of selecting say, "News," tap on **Smart Home**, then **Turn on scene** or **Control Device** as the case may be. However, take note that your Smart Home Device must have been configured with Alexa before now.

From the list of Smart Home Devices that you've added to Alexa, choose the one you want to add to Alexa routine and what function or how you want it to work in the union. **Add** to continue. You may choose to adjust again the **time** and **day** that you want the action/function of the Smart Home Device to be triggered. You can also add more actions to the routine. Tap on Create to finish up.

How to Add Music to a Routine

It's rather easy to create a routine with your favorite music. A music routine can pass for an alarm if you create it using scheduled time and day. To get started, from the Alexa app, add a music action for the condition that you want your routine to occur by tapping on the **plus**  icon. On the next screen, pick a song by typing in the song title. Next, select the **Music Provider**. Your music could come from your music library, Pandora, Amazon, Spotify, TuneIn or iHeartRadio. **Preview** your selection and **Add** it to the routine.

Having Alexa say something in a Routine

Alexa can say a phrase when a routine is triggered. Such phrases could be a welcome home message, a compliment, a goodbye, good night or good morning message, a birthday wish, etc.

To get started, from the Alexa app, add a music action for the condition that you want your routine to occur by tapping on the **plus**  icon. On the next screen, select a category and pick a phrase from there then **Add** your selection.

Once you've confirmed your selection, select from the list the device you would like your phrase to be played from, and you are done.

Chapter 7

Alexa Communication

Alexa can keep the household, friends, and family always connected. It can work as an intercom device within the house or used as a standard telephone conversation device over the Internet. It can initiate an instant two-way communication between rooms or send an announcement from one room to the rest within the house. You can also use Alexa to send a message or call anyone from your Alexa contact for free using your Alexa-enabled device or via the Alexa app installed on your smartphone or tablet. You can also send e-mails, make and receive Skype calls once your e-mail and Skype account are linked to Alexa.

To get started with Alexa communication, open the Alexa mobile application, and on the homepage, tap the Communication icon and begin to set up your Alexa for communication if you have not done so before this time.

To get this completed without problems, make sure your smartphone is running the latest Amazon Alexa application (9.0 or higher for iOS and 5.0 or higher for Android). Fire tablets can also make calls.

How to send SMS

Once you've set up your Alexa app for conversations or communication, you can begin to send SMS to your Alexa contacts. You can send messages to family and friends using your Echo device or the Alexa app.

From your Alexa app, tap on the **Communication** tab then, **Contacts** icon (see top right-hand side of the page). Tap on **My Profile** and under **Permission**, toggle on **Send SMS**, and you are good to go. Allow Alexa to send and read SMS. This is done only once as part of the setup process. Next, import all contacts from your phone to Alexa. In future, you simply tap the message icon to see supported contacts that you can send a message to instantly.

Subsequently, when on the **Contacts** page, you can manage your contacts by tapping the three dots **: Add Contact** to add new contacts within the Alexa application or **Block** any contact from reaching you via Alexa. You can also toggle **Enable** under **Import Contacts** to allow Alexa to update your contacts from your phonebook from time to time.

The command here is simple: “Alexa, send a text message,” “Alexa, send an SMS.” Alexa would then request for a contact within your Alexa app. Give Alexa a contact name, say your message and leave the rest for Alexa.

You can also save Alexa some stress by using a command such as: “Alexa, send a text message to {your Alexa app contact name} or “Alexa, send an SMS to {your Alexa app contact name},” or “Alexa, message {your Alexa app contact name}.”

When you have a new message, you would see a dot on the Communication icon 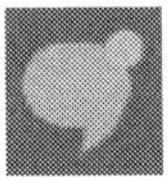 on the home page or indicator light on the Echo device. To hear your new message, say, “Alexa, play my messages.”

Note: (a) Your SMS recipient’s mobile operating system must also be Android else this won’t go well; (b) You can’t send an SMS to 911, or groups; (c) You can’t also send an MMS with this setup.

How to make Video / Audio Calls with Amazon Alexa

You can make free calls to other Echo devices or contacts on your Alexa app that support this feature. You want to try? Okay! Launch your Alexa app and tap on the **Communication**  icon. Tap on the **Contacts**  icon. Grant Alexa all necessary permissions if doing this for the first time. All your contacts would be displayed here. You can tap on any to see if they can receive a call from Alexa. Tapping on any contact shows options to make audio or video call. Subsequently, you can easily tap on the **Call**  icon once you are on the **Communication** page to start making calls.

Using voice command, you can say, "Alexa, call Michael Smith," "Alexa, video off" [that's if she's trying to video call by default]. You are done talking? Then say, "Alexa, end call." You can as well tap on the **Hang Up** icon on the screen if using an Echo device with a screen to end a call or simply say, "Alexa, hang up." To answer a call, say, "Alexa, answer."

To answer or ignore your Alexa-to-Alexa incoming calls to your Echo device, say, "Alexa, answer," or "Alexa, ignore." You can also use the Do-Not-Disturb feature to block or ignore calls.

How to Link your Skype Account to Alexa to Make and Receive Skype Calls

Amazon Alexa keeps becoming more and more interesting with each passing day. Now, you can call and receive calls from your Skype contacts using Amazon Alexa.

To get started, you would need:
(a) A compatible Amazon Alexa-enabled device.

(b) Your call recipient must update their Skype application to the latest version.

(c) Your Alexa communication must be enabled. Obviously, you have done this by now.

To set up your Skype communication with Alexa, get your Skype login details handy and in the Alexa application, go to **Menu** and then **Settings** and under **Alexa Preferences**, select **Communications**. Under **Accounts**, tap the **Plus** sign (+) against **Skype** to **Sign In** with your details and connect your account. When Alexa attempt to redirect, select a browser on your phone and continue to configure your Skype account for Alexa. Once the configuration is complete, you can begin calling and receiving your Skype calls.

The general format for calling your Skype contacts is “Alexa, Skype {recipient’s Skype ID},” e.g., “Alexa, Skype Michael.” However, you can also say, “Alexa, call Michael on Skype,” or “Alexa, call 206-111-0334.” To answer an incoming call, simply say, “Alexa, answer.”

Skype rewards with free calling minutes when you connect your Skype account to Alexa. Existing Skype subscription can also work with Amazon Alexa.

The Drop In feature

This feature allows you to start an audio or video conversation with another user of Alexa Drop-In enabled device. You can also watch and/or listen to what another user is doing depending on what Echo device they are using. As a result, you can easily use this feature to monitor happenings around your house. You can also refer to it as an intercom.

The Alexa Drop-In feature can allow someone to drop-in on you unannounced through your Echo device. When an Echo device with a screen drops in on another Echo device with a screen, you get a video feed. Since this comes unannounced, you can choose to disable it to avoid someone popping into your privacy.

Due to its sensitive nature, it is **Disabled** by default.

To enable [or disable] it, launch your Alexa mobile app and tap the **Menu** 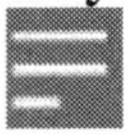 icon, go to **Settings** and select the device you want to enable or disable the drop-in function. Tap the **Drop-In** menu and tune it the way you want from there. You have options to enable [On], allow it to work within your home or disable [Off] it completely. To try this out after enabling the feature, say, "Alexa, drop-in on {Echo device name}."

To drop-in on someone using the Alexa app, tap the **Communication**  icon then tap **Drop In** and select the Echo device you want to drop-in from there.

Some useful invocation phrases:
You can start with "Alexa, drop in," or "Alexa, drop in on Computer" or "Alexa, hang up" to end a drop in session.

How to Make an Announcement with Alexa

With Amazon Alexa, you can simply announce a message from one point of the house to the rest of the rooms. It's a kind of one-way intercom where you send a message to all Alexa-enabled devices within the house using your voice. When announcement is sent, Alexa plays a short alert on connected Echo devices then begin to announce the message with the sender's voice.

Maybe you want to tell everyone to come down for dinner, you can say, "Alexa, announce "Can you come for dinner?"" You can also use the word 'broadcast' instead of 'announce.' For example, "Alexa, broadcast that we are late."
To make an announcement using the Alexa app, open the application and tap the **Communication**  icon then **Announce** . On the ensuing screen, type your message or hit the **Microphone**  icon to say your message. Finally, tap the arrow  icon to make your announcement.

<u>Notes</u>:
(a) Mobile devices can only send announcements but cannot receive. Announcements only play on Echo devices.

(b) Tap the **Menu** icon, and then **Settings** and under **Alexa Preferences**, tap **Communication** and select your device to manage the announcement settings for that device.

(c) Enabling a Do-Not-Disturb on an Echo device stops announcement from coming to the device. However, you can still make an announcement from the device.

How to link your Email to Amazon Alexa

You can link your email accounts and have Alexa help you to manage it. Before continuing, note that anyone that gain access to your smartphone where the Alexa application is installed or your Echo devices can access your emails. You can connect up to 3 emails addresses to your Alexa account. Your adult Household Member can also do same. You can set and use a voice PIN to safeguard your email from unauthorized access.

To link an account, launch the Alexa app and go to **Settings**, tap **Email & Calendar**. See the list of providers supported by Alexa and choose one to set up. Supply login details and grant Alexa access. Alexa reports on your email activities for the last 24 hrs.

Some useful invocations phrases
To see **new** emails:
"Alexa, what's my mail?"
"Alexa, open my mail."
"Alexa, did {sender name} send me any email?"

To **read/hear** content:
"Alexa, play new messages"

To **reply**:
"Alexa, reply."

To **skip** an email:
"Alexa, skip."
To **delete**:
"Alexa, delete it."

Using a skill to send/receive SMS, make calls, on/off Bluetooth, locate your phone, on/off WiFi, etc.

Enabling the Mastermind skills ("Alexa, enable Mastermind" can even help you to do more in sending/receiving SMS, making calls, on/off Bluetooth, locating your phone, on/off WiFi, etc.

From here, you can say something like: "Alexa, ask Mastermind to send a text to John Paul," "Alexa, ask Mastermind to ring my phone," "Alexa, ask Mastermind to call Kelly,"

“Alexa, ask Mastermind to turn on WiFi on <device name>,” “Alexa, ask Mastermind to turn on Bluetooth on <device name>,” “Alexa, ask Mastermind to read new emails,” “Alexa, donate $50 to Doctors Without Borders.” Other charities include; ASPCA, America Heart Association, One Laptop Per Child, Wikimedia Foundation, etc.

.

Chapter 8

Alexa Entertainment

Alexa can give you an entertaining experience you never imagined. From music, radio stations, podcasts to books, games, movies, or jokes, Alexa have it all. Simply knock and it shall be opened unto you, I mean ask!

Alexa Music Services

You can link up to music services such as Amazon Music, Spotify, Apple Music, Pandora, iHeartRadio, TuneIn, and more. Once you are done linking up a music service, you can only sit back tell Alexa what you want from it with your voice.

To get started with your music service in the Alexa, tap the **Music & Books**  icon. Scroll down and tap **More Music Streaming Services** to setup your music services on your Echo device. Select your favorite **Music Provider** from the dropdown and link your account with them. To **disconnect** from a Music Service, select **Unlink account from Alexa** against the music service you want to disconnect from your Amazon Alexa.

Useful invocation phrases:
Basic controls:
Playback
"Alexa, shuffle."
"Alexa, stop."
"Alexa, pause."
"Alexa, play."
"Alexa, resume."
"Alexa, skip."
"Alexa, next."

Volume
"Alexa, volume up."
"Alexa, volume 5."

Equalizer
"Alexa, set the bass to 5."
"Alexa, turn up the treble."
"Alexa, reset the equalizer."

A little advanced:
"Alexa, play latest track by {artist name},"
"Alexa, play songs similar to 70s."

Music services:
"Alexa, play [artist name / song title / album title / playlist name]"

"Alexa, play {radio station name} on {Music Service},"

Even more:
"Alexa, play Prime Playlist."

"Alexa, play {song title} from {Music Service}."

To create a playlist:
"Alexa, create a playlist."

To play from a playlist:
"Alexa, play playlist Country Christmas."

To add songs to a playlist:
"Alexa, add [song / artist name / album] to <playlist name>."

Note:
(a) If you are not comfortable with explicit songs, in the Alexa app, navigate: Settings => Music => Explicit Filter. Toggle Explicit Filter On. Using voice, you can say, "Alexa, block explicit music" to turn it on or "Alexa, stop blocking explicit music" to turn it off.

(b) Where you are unable to launch some Music Services due to explicit filtering, please turn off the feature and try again.

Amazon Music

Prime and Amazon Music Unlimited members or subscribers can make good choices of music from Alexa. To start a trial of Amazon Music Unlimited, say, "Alexa, start my trial of Amazon Music Unlimited."

To set up your Amazon Music Service, launch your Alexa app and tap the **Music & Book** 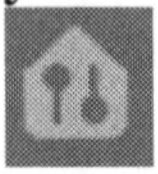 icon then select **Music**. Find all Music Services listed under Music. Select **Amazon Music**. On the Playlist tab, you can choose from **Decade, Artist, Genres or Mood & Activities** then a **Category**. Finally, choose a Playlist to play. Control your playback as desired.

Useful / pattern of invocation phrases:
"Alexa, play music."
"Alexa, play music that have just been released."
"Alexa, play more of this nature."
"Alexa, play the new Rihana's album."
"Alexa, play the song with the lyrics, 'love is all that matters.'"
"Alexa, set an alarm with a song from Adele every [Thursday / everyday] at 5:00am."
"Alexa, wake me to Beyonce's music."
"Alexa, play latest hits in New York."
"Alexa, play a party pop music."
"Alexa, play any music suited for cooking."
"Alexa, repeat the songs you played last Sunday."

iHeartRadio

To setup your iHeartRadio on Alexa, sign up on http://iheart.com using a Computer, and sign in with same login details on Alexa app via Settings => Music & Books => Music => iHeartRadio.

You can listen to over 850+ stations on iHeartRadio on your Echo Show. Content includes talk, music, news, sports, etc. Well, you should have your favorite station in mind but if you don't, head over to http://iheart.com and look at some channels there. You can choose to search by location or genre. To play any channel of your choice, use the format: "Alexa, play {radio station's name} on iHeartRadio." Example, "Alexa, play Kiss FM on iHeartRadio," or "Alexa, play Kiss FM on iHeartRadio on Group 1" where Group 1 is your Echo speaker group name for a Multi-Room Music setup. To stop playing, say, "Alexa, stop."

Spotify

Like the iHeartRadio, use your PC to create an account with Spotify then come back to Alexa app and log in to the music service with your login details via Setting => Music & Books => Music => Spotify.

If you are on Spotify Premium, you can use the Spotify app on your smartphone or tablet device as a remote. This means you should have a **Spotify Connect** subscription.

From here, you can say, "Alexa, Connect to Spotify" to enable your Spotify Connect subscription or "Alexa, play {genre} on Spotify."

Pandora

Sign up on http://pandora.com using a Computer and on the Alexa app, go to Settings => Music & Books => Music => Pandora => Enable. Sign in with your Pandora account information.

To request a song:
"Alexa, play {artist name} radio from Pandora." Where the song isn't available, a station would be created for you.

To vote a song:
"Alexa give a [Thumb Up / Thumb Down] to this song."

To control playback:
"Alexa, [play / stop] music on Pandora."

To skip a song:
"Alexa, skip this song."

To control volume:
"Alexa, turn volume [down / up]."

To know what's playing:
"Alexa, what's playing?"

Pandora Premium users can request a playlist, specific song or album to be played for them, e.g., "Alexa, play One Dance by Drake on Pandora."

To disable Pandora on Alexa
On the Alexa app, go to Settings => Music & Books => Music => Pandora => Disable.

SiriusXM

Follow a similar method like the above to **Enable** SiriusXM on Alexa. Once enabled, **Link your Account** with your login details. To learn more, go to http://siriusxm.com.

TuneIn

In the Alexa app, tap on the **Menu** icon then Skills. Use the search bar to search for and **Enable** TuneIn Live Skill. To use your voice to enable TuneIn, say, "Alexa, open TuneIn Live" and say "Yes" to her prompt.

You can stream news, music, sport and podcasts from TuneIn. TuneIn works with content providers such as NHL, MLB, NBA, NFL, Al Jazeera, MSNBC, CNBC, Newsy, etc.

Deezer

Deezer is a premium music service on Alexa. You can listen to Deezer using an Alexa-enabled device in the US, UK, Canada, Germany, Ireland, New Zealand, and Australia. Sign up for a paid account on http://deezer.com.

Deezer is already listed on Alexa and all you need to do is to activate and start using it. To get started, tap on **Music & Books**  icon from the Alexa homepage and select **Deezer** and subsequently tap **Enable** to initiate the activation process. Enter your login details to fully activate it on Alexa.

Apple Music

Alexa cannot directly link to Apple Music like other service but you can still work around and get her to play your Apple Music. One way to go about this is to pair your smartphone with your Echo Dot and use the Echo Dot as a Bluetooth speaker. Once your smartphone is linked to the Echo Dot, use it to play your Apple Music.

You can still have Alexa to exercise basic control over the playback. To disconnect your smartphone from the Echo device, say, "Alexa, disconnect."

Setting your Default Music Service

A default Music Service attends to your music request any time you need it. When your default Music Service is set, you can simply call for music without necessarily specifying what service should fulfill the request. A request such as, "Alexa, play music" is going to be handled by your default Music Service. Here, you don't specify where the music should come from (e.g., "Alexa, play Ignition by R. Kelly ~~on Pandora~~"), so Alexa simply starts playing from your default Music Service.

However, where a default music service is not set, you would have to specify which service should handle your request. Your request would always have to take the format: "Alexa, play {song / album title / genre / ...} on {music service}."

To set your default music service in the Alexa app, tap the **Menu** 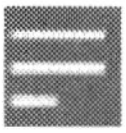 icon then **Settings**. Under **Settings**, tap **Alexa Preferences, Music** and under **Account Settings**, **Select Your Default Music Service** and tap **Done**.

Multi-Room Music with Amazon Echo Device

This feature is supported by all Amazon Echos with the exception of the Echo Tap and Fire TV. To get started, connect your Amazon Echo speakers on the same network. Apart from having your Echo speakers all connected to the same WiFi connection, you'll also need at best an Amazon Music Unlimited or a Prime Music Account. While you can setup a Multi-Room Music with a Prime Music account, an Amazon Music Unlimited account is nevertheless the best for this.

A Multi-Room Music setup with a **Prime Music** account can only enable you to stream a music channel (e.g., Pandora only) at a time to a speaker group, while a **Music Unlimited with a Family Plan** can stream multi-music channels (e.g., iHeartRadio and SiriusXM) at the same time to different speaker groups. However, take note that Multi-Room Music setup does not work with speakers connected over Bluetooth.

To get started with **Multi-Room Music** setup, click on **Devices** 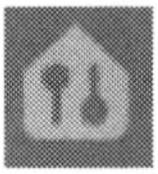 from the homepage to see controls for Smart Home Devices. Tap the **plus** sign , and then **Add Multi-Room Music Speakers**. Name your group either by choosing from system suggestions or inputting your custom name. Select the Echo speakers you want to use in forming a group. Once done, tap Save. Note that a speaker can't be added to two or more groups. You can always remove your Echo speaker from **its group** under **Speaker Groups** in **Devices** 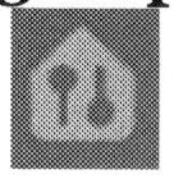 .

Once setup is completed for the group, it's ready for use. Simply say, "Alexa, play music on 'Group 1" where Group 1 is your Echo speaker group name. Here, Alexa plays from the default music service. You can also say, "Alexa, play SiriusXM on 'Group 1." You can stop the playback from any Echo.

To control which speaker within a group plays what, use the format: "Alexa, play TuneIn on 'Group 1' and play SiriusXM on 'Group 2" where 'Group 1' and 'Group 2' are your Echo speaker group names where your default music service is set to Amazon Music Unlimited.

More useful invocations:
"Alexa, play [artist / playlist name] on {Echo speaker group name}."

"Alexa, play {name of radio station} on Pandora on {Echo speaker group name}."

"Alexa, play music everywhere."

Radio and Podcasts

Listen to Radio and Podcast on News, Finance, Science, Tech & Design, Pop Culture, etc.

Even when you don't have any specific podcast genre or Radio station, Alexa can recommend something to you. For Radio, you can say, "Alexa, recommend a radio station for me," or "Alexa, play Z100," where Z100 is your radio station.

For podcast, where you know the title of the podcast, you can say, "Alexa, [show / play] the podcast {podcast title/name}," or "Alexa, recommend a {genre} podcast for me" or simply tell her to play a podcast for you.

Playing Games with Alexa

Feeling bored? Alexa can help with fun games. To get started, you'll have to enable the skills—I mean your games, and it's easy too. As usual, to enable a skill in Alexa, launch the Alexa app and tap on **Skills & Games** from the **Menu**. Tap on **Game, Trivia & Accessories** and browse through the games there. Once you find something that you love, tap on **Enable Skill**. Got some games idea? Create those ideas via Alexa Blueprints (*see* section Alexa Blueprint—How to Create Custom Skills for Amazon Alexa).

Some recommendations include; Jeopardy, Price It Right, Twenty Questions, Bingo, Game Of Lists, Spelling Bee, Song Quiz, Screen Test, Millionaire Quiz Game, Code Guess, Letter Clutter, Guess My name, Yes Sire, The Magic Door, etc. To launch or play a game once enabled, say, "Alexa, open [or play] {skill/game name}."

One more thing: you can enable Twitch to help you with updates on your favorite players or IRL channels. You can say, "Alexa, ask Twitch which player is playing {game name}," or "Alexa, ask Twitch to recommend an IRL channel."

Taking your gaming experience to another level with the Echo Button

You can link up your Echo button to have a hands-on gaming experience with Alexa.

Once your button is linked to Alexa, you can ask her what games you can play with the Echo button. However, you can start with Bandit Buttons or Trivial Pursuit Tap. For more suggestions, say, "Alexa, can you recommend a game for my Echo Buttons?"

Alexa for Kids

Alexa is fun for the family. Allow the children also to have a feel of her like you do.

Few recommendations include; Christmas Kindness, the Magic Door, Spelling Bee, Ditty, Curiosity, Superheroes, Knock Knock Jokes, Short Bedtime Story, Cat Facts, Dog Facts, Dinosaur Facts, Guess the Number, Twenty Questions, State Capital Quiz, Earplay, Bingo, Laugh Box, Complibot, Pikachu Talk, Sheep Count, Kids News, Quick Snacks, 4A Fart, Panda Rescue, Sesame Street, Escape the Room, Freeze Dancers, See Say, Science Buddy, True or False, Eco Hacks, Heads Up, etc.

You can use this format to invoke any of these skills: “Alexa, open <skill name>” or “Alexa, start <skill name>.”

Fun time with Alexa

Do you know that Alexa can tell you jokes, stories or sing for you? Even today, she is much ready for you. Just say, “Alexa, tell me some jokes,” or “Alexa, tell me a Christmas joke.” Maybe you want to know more about Alexa, you can say, “Alexa, who are you?” “Alexa, are you okay?” “Alexa, do you like red color?” You like poems or stories? Well, you can try, “Alexa, tell me a nice poem” or “Alexa, sing a love song for me.”

Alexa can read your Kindle or Audible Books

Alexa can conveniently read Text-to-Speech supported eBooks in your Kindle Library. To get started, tap on the **Music & Book**  icon located on the Alexa homepage. In the Kindle Library, you can see all your eBooks. Select any one and choose a device for it. Whether the book was shared with you, you purchased or borrowed them, Alexa can attempt reading them for you. It doesn’t matter if you’ve read the book from another device, Alexa can pick up from there. This is made possible by the Whispersync for Voice technology supported by Alexa.

Useful invocations phrases:
Reading eBooks

To see your books:
“Alexa, show my Kindle Books.”

To start book reading:
“Alexa, play {book title} from Kindle Library”

To control playback: “Alexa, [stop / pause / resume / skip / go ahead / next chapter].”

To jump to another chapter: “Alexa, read <chapter number>.”

Listening to audiobooks

Listening to an audiobook:
“Alexa, read <book title>”

To control playback:
“Alexa, [stop / pause / resume my book]”

To go backward or forward by 30 seconds: “Alexa, go back / go forward].”

To jump to another chapter: “Alexa, [next / previous] chapter. Or “Alexa, go to chapter {#}.”

Restart a chapter:
“Alexa, restart.”

Stop after time count: “Alexa, stop reading in {#} minutes” or “Alexa, stop reading in {#} hour.”

To have Alexa read a title from Audible: “Alexa, read {book title} from Audible.”

To get information about free books: “Alexa, what’s free on Audible today?”

Full Alexa Easter eggs

"Alexa, do you really want to hurt me?"
"Alexa, what is love?"
"Alexa, who is the real slim shady?"
"Alexa, who let the dogs out?"
"Alexa, open the pod bay doors."
"Alexa, surely you can't be serious."
"Alexa, to be or not to be."
"Alexa, who is the fairest of them all?"
"Alexa, who loves ya baby?"
"Alexa, who you gonna call?"
"Alexa, who is the walrus?"
"Alexa, do you have any brothers or sisters?"
"Alexa, do you know the muffin man?"
"Alexa, how much do you weigh?"
"Alexa, how tall are you?"
"Alexa, where are you from?"
"Alexa, do you want to fight?"
"Alexa, do you want to play a game?"
"Alexa, I think you're funny."
"Alexa, where in the world is Carmen sandiego?"
"Alexa, where's Waldo?"
"Alexa, do you know the way to San Jose?"
"Alexa, where have all the flowers gone?"
"Alexa, what's in name?"
"Alexa, what does the fox say? (Multiple answers)"
"Alexa, when am I going to die?"
"Alexa, I want the truth!"
"Alexa, make me breakfast."
"Alexa, why did the chicken cross the road?"
"Alexa, where are my keys? (Ask twice)."
"Alexa, can you give me some money? (Ask twice)."
"Alexa, knock knock."
"Alexa, what are you wearing?"

"Alexa, good morning."
"Alexa, give me an Easter egg."
"Alexa, beam me up."
"Alexa, tell me a joke."
"Alexa, set phasers to kill."
"Alexa, my name is Inigo Montoya."
"Alexa, I want the truth."
"Alexa, show me the money."
"Alexa, party on, Wayne."
"Alexa, party time!"
"Alexa, what's the first rule of Fight Club?"
"Alexa, surely you can't be serious."
"Alexa, are you SkyNet?"
"Alexa, when am I going to die?"
"Alexa, open the pod bay doors."
"Alexa, nice to see you, to see you..."
"Alexa, what is your quest?"
"Alexa, this is a dead parrot."
"Alexa, don't mention the war."
"Alexa, what is your cunning plan?"
"Alexa, what are the laws of robotics?"
"Alexa, I am your father."
"Alexa, who lives in a pineapple under the sea?"
"Alexa, what is the loneliest number?"
"Alexa, how many roads must a man walk down?"
"Alexa, all your base are belong to us."
"Alexa, how much is that doggie in the window?"

"Alexa, Romeo, Romeo wherefore art thou Romeo?"
"Alexa, beam me up."
"Alexa, how much wood can a woodchuck chuck if a woodchuck could chuck wood?"
"Alexa, define supercalifragilisticexpialodocious."
"Alexa, who's your daddy?"
"Alexa, Tea. Earl Grey. Hot."
"Alexa, what is the meaning of life?"
"Alexa, what does the Earth weigh?"
"Alexa, when is the end of the world?"
"Alexa, is there a Santa?"
"Alexa, make me a sandwich."
"Alexa, what is the best tablet?"
"Alexa, what is your favorite color?"
"Alexa, what is your quest?"
"Alexa, who won best actor Oscar in 1973?"
"Alexa, what is your quest?"
"Alexa, what is the airspeed velocity of an unladen swallow?"
"Alexa, where do babies come from?"
"Alexa, do you have a boyfriend?"
"Alexa, which comes first: the chicken or the egg?"
"Alexa, may the force be with you."
"Alexa, do aliens exist?"
"Alexa, how many licks does it take to get to the center of a tootsie pop?"
"Alexa, what are you going to do today?"
"Alexa, where do you live?"
"Alexa, do you want to build a snowman?"

"Alexa, rock paper scissors."
"Alexa rock paper scissors lizard spock."
"Alexa, party time!"
"Alexa, party on, Wayne."
"Alexa, is the cake a lie?"
"Alexa, how do I get rid of a dead body?"
"Alexa, are you sky net?"
"Alexa, your mother was a hamster"
"Alexa, set phasers to kill."
"Alexa, roll a die."
"Alexa, random number between "x" and "y"."
"Alexa, random fact"
"Alexa, tell me a joke"
"Alexa, heads or tails?"
"Alexa, mac or pc?"
"Alexa, show me the money."
"Alexa, what is the sound of one hand clapping?"
"Alexa, give me a hug."
"Alexa, are you lying?"
"Alexa, my name is Inigo Montoya."
"Alexa, how many angels can dance on the head of a pin?"
"Alexa, see you later alligator."
"Alexa, what's the answer to life, the universe, and everything?"
"Alexa, what are the laws of robotics?"
"Alexa, are there UFOs?"
"Alexa, is there life on Mars?"
"Alexa, take me to your leader."
"Alexa, these aren't the droids you're looking for."
"Alexa, I've seen things you people wouldn't believe."
"Alexa, does this unit have a soul?"
"Alexa, ya feel me?"

"Alexa, wakey wakey?"
"Alexa, is there life on other planets?"
"Alexa, how old are you?"
"Alexa, are you okay?"
"Alexa, did you get my email?"
"Alexa, do you dream?"
"Alexa, do you believe in love at first sight?"
"Alexa, where did you grow up?"
"Alexa, what is your favorite food?"
"Alexa, what's your birthday? (Multiple)."
"Alexa, are you alive?"
"Alexa, have you ever seen the rain?
"Alexa, were you sleeping?"
"Alexa, will pigs fly?"
"Alexa, do you have a last name?"
"Alexa, are you stupid?"
"Alexa, are you smart?"
"Alexa, am I hot?"
"Alexa, are you real? (Multiple)."
"Alexa, do I need an umbrella today?"
"Alexa, did you fart?"
"Alexa, say, "Cheese!" (Multiple)."
"Alexa, what do you mean I'm funny?"
"Alexa, who is Eliza?"
"Alexa, what's black and white and red all over? (Multiple)."
"Alexa, say something."
"Alexa, say something funny."
"Alexa, are you my mommy?"
"Alexa, flip a coin."
"Alexa, marco..."
"Alexa, I'm sick."

"Alexa, I've fallen, and I can't get up!"
"Alexa, I'm sick of your **** (any 4 letter expletive)."
"Alexa, You're such a/an ***** (any colorfully descriptive word)."
"Alexa, ha ha! (say the words)."
"Alexa, speak!"
"Alexa, welcome!"
"Alexa, what's your sign?"
"Alexa, I'm bored."
"Alexa, you are so intelligent."
"Alexa, Hello HAL."
"Alexa, Who's better, you or Siri?"
"Alexa, Sorry!"
"Alexa, We all scream for ice cream!"
"Alexa, can you lie?"
"Alexa, how are you doing?"
"Alexa, what do you think about Google?"
"Alexa, what do you think about Apple? (Multiple)."
"Alexa, what do you think about Google Glass? (Multiple)."
"Alexa, Happy Birthday."
"Alexa, Cheers!"
"Alexa, say you're sorry (multiple)."
"Alexa, I'll be back (ode to Schwarzenegger)."
"Alexa, All's well that ends well."
"Alexa, what is the Seven Wonders of the World?"
"Alexa, you suck! (Multiple)."
"Alexa, how do you spell f_ck|sh_t|mf|c_cks_cker|t_ts?"
"Alexa, shit!"
"Alexa, Can you smell that?"

Holiday Greetings
"Alexa, Merry Christmas."
"Alexa, Happy Christmas."
"Alexa, Happy Holidays."
"Alexa, Happy Thanksgiving."
"Alexa, Happy Halloween."
"Alexa, Happy Valentine's Day."
"Alexa, Happy St. Patrick's Day."
"Alexa, Happy Mother's Day."
"Alexa, Happy Father's Day."
"Alexa, Happy New Year."
"Alexa, Happy Easter."
"Alexa, Happy Ramadan."
"Alexa, Happy Hanukkah."
"Alexa, Happy Kwanzaa."

Chapter 9

Discover Alexa's Productivity Prowess

From adding an event to your calendar, shopping or to-do list, setting day-saving reminders, alarms and timers, Alexa is here to help while you focus on other things. You can use a voice command to cancel or set countdown timers and manage settings in the Alexa app. It could be a named or countdown timer—as you wish. You can also set your alarms and reminders using your voice or the Alexa app. There's even more that you can do with Alexa. Find out!

How to set a Timer

Alexa can help you set up a named, sleep or multiple timers just with your command.

A **named timer** could sound like:
"Alexa, set a **sleep timer** for 90 minutes" or
"Alexa, set a lunch timer for 35 minutes."

You can also set **multiple timers** by saying, "Alexa, set a second timer for 10 minutes."

You want to check timer status?
"Alexa, what are my timers?" or

"Alexa, what time is left on the lunch timer?"

While a **countdown timer** could sound like: "Alexa, stop playing in 50 minutes" or "Alexa, set a timer for 20 minutes."

While your timer is running, you can say, “Alexa, [cancel / stop] sleep timer,” “Alexa, what time is remaining in sleep timer?” or “Alexa, what time is remaining in my timer?”

To cancel a timer, say, "Alexa, cancel the lunch timer" or "Alexa, cancel the 20-minute timer."

How to set a Reminder

Ask Alexa to remind you of your important tasks or even so you don’t miss them. Standard format: “Alexa, add a reminder about {name of activity} by {time} {when}” e.g., “Alexa, add a reminder about going to church by 6:00 am tomorrow.”

How to set an Alarm

To set an alarm for any particular time, say, "Alexa, set an alarm for 4 a.m.," "Alexa, wake me up by 4 a.m. in the morning."

If you want to rather set a music alarm, you can say, "Alexa, wake me up to [artist name /

song title / genre / playlist name / album] at 4 a.m.," or "Alexa, wake me up to Urban FM at 4 a.m on TuneIn"

Maybe you want to set alarm on repeat mode, you can say, "Alexa, set a repeating alarm for weekdays at 4 a.m."

You want to find out about next alarm? "Alexa, when is my next alarm?"

You want to cancel an alarm? "Alexa, cancel my alarm for 4 p.m."

You want to snooze an alarm? "Alexa, snooze."

To setup your Reminders, Alarms or Timers manually, go to Reminders & Alarms under Menu in the Alexa app.

Linking your Calendar to Alexa

Alexa supports Apple (Calendar only), Google (Email and Calendar), Microsoft (Email and Calendar) and Microsoft Exchange (Calendar only) through Office 365 and Outlook. To make it happen, on the Alexa app, go to **Settings**, scroll down and tap on **Email & Calendar**. Select your preferred service and **Connect your Account** supplying your login credentials (if necessary). Grant Alexa necessary permissions and finally, your account email and calendar are added.

To keep things easy, work with just a Calendar. Tap on the checkbox against the calendar that you've setup earlier then go Back (see arrow at top left). Continue to configure your chosen calendar for Alexa in Email & Calendar. Finally, you are set. Remember that household members can also access your Email and Calendar.

At this point, you can **add events** to your calendar using the format: "Alexa, add {event name} to my calendar by {time} on {when}." Example, "Alexa, add meeting to my calendar by 2pm tomorrow," or "Alexa, add travel to my calendar by 5am on Monday."

To **reschedule** an event, you can say, "Alexa, move {event name} from {old time or date/time} to {new time or date/time}."

To find out what's on your calendar, just say, "Alexa, what event do I have on my calendar today?" or "Alexa, what's next on my calendar?"

Creating and Managing your Shopping / To-do List

Amazon list comes with two default lists: Shopping and To-do. You can easily start adding items to these lists through your Alexa app or using your voice. You can also create custom lists and add items to them or access your Amazon Alexa lists using 3rd party applications such as AnyList, Any.do and Todoist.

To create a custom list using the Alexa app, tap on the **Menu**  icon and select **Lists**. Select **Create List** and type in a name for your list. Tap the **Add** (+) icon or tap the enter button on your mobile keypad to create your list. You can start adding items to your list immediately. Your custom list would be listed under **My Lists in Lists.**

In a similar manner, you can tap on any of the default lists and items to them.

Alternatively, you can use your voice to create a list by saying, “Alexa, create a {list name} list.” To add items to your list, you can say, “Alexa, add {item name} to my [shopping / to-do / {custom list name}] list,” or “Alexa, remove {item name} from my [shopping / to-do / {custom list name}] list.”

More useful invocations:
To delete a list: “Alexa, remove {item name or number} in my {list name}.”

To find out what's on your list: "Alexa, what's on my [shopping / to-do / {custom list name}] list."

To clear a list: "Alexa, clear my [shopping / to-do / {custom list name}] list."

To manage your list using a 3rd party list service, go to **Settings** and tap on **Lists**. Select a list service from the list that appears and **Enable to Use** the skill. Follow through to configure the service. To disable the skill, go back to **Lists** under **Settings**, tap on it and **Disable** Skill.

Simple Mathematics with Alexa

Alexa can handle simple Mathematics (especially for your kids) such as multiplication, basic addition, subtraction or division. Alexa can also give the value of Mathematical constants or help you with simple conversions (e.g., currency, metrics, etc.), e.g., "Alexa, how much is 50 Pounds in US Dollars?"

The skill, 1-2-3 Math can also help your kids to learn Math even faster. It tests one's ability to add, subtract, multiply, divide, compare, etc. It works in three modes: easy, medium & hard. You may need a Calculator to meet up with allotted time. To enable this skill, say, "Alexa, enable one two three."

Random Facts from Alexa

Simply say, "Alexa tell me some facts" or "Alexa, tell me some interesting things" and you'll be shocked with facts from Alexa.

Alternatively, you can enable a skill for random facts. To enable random facts skills, say, "Alexa, [start / open / launch] Random Facts." You can request for facts across categories such as money, random, Disney, weather, Dinosaur, number, food, today, world, etc. You can also enable additional extras with a premium subscription.

Get Financial Information from Alexa

When asked financial questions, Alexa searches through connected services to supply answer to your question. It may take up to 15 minutes to get response.

You can ask questions about Stock Prices, Index Values, Commodities and Foreign Exchange Rates from the following Providers.

[1] Dow Jones Indices, United States.
[2] S&P Indices, United States.
[3] NASDAQ, United States.
[4] Borsa Italiana, Europe.
[5] London Stock Exchange, Europe.
[6] Euronext Amsterdam, Europe.

[7] Euronext Brussels, Europe.
[8] Euronext Paris, Europe.
[9] Madrid Stock Exchange, Europe.
[10] National Stock Exchange, India.
[11] Toronto Stock Exchange, Canada.
[12] New Zealand Stock Exchange, New Zealand.

Get Medical Information from Alexa

Alexa continues to improve and becoming even more sophisticated. Now, you can ask Alexa some medical questions bordering on symptoms, causes and treatments from trusted sources such as Mayo Clinic, CDC, NIH, Disease Ontology Database, Wikipedia and Wikidata.

Important Notice: Medical information provided by Alexa is only for informational purpose and should not be used as a standard for treatment. If you have medical emergency, get to a nearby hospital immediately or call your Doctor.

Get Information from Wikipedia

While you can do this through the Browser, you can also use your voice to fetch information from Wikipedia by saying,

"Alexa, Wikipedia <subject>," e.g., "Alexa, Wikipedia Albert Einstein."

Information on Nearby Places: Businesses and Restaurants

Get information about shops, local restaurants, and other businesses. It's important that your address in Settings is correct and complete especially for this purpose. Alexa uses information mostly from Yelp to deliver on your requests.

To search for restaurants or businesses nearby:
"Alexa, which [restaurants / businesses] close to me"

To see top-rated restaurants/businesses close to you:
"Alexa, what top-rated [restaurants / businesses] are close to me?"

Get address of a restaurant/business close to you:
"Alexa, find the address of [restaurants / businesses] close to me."

To get phone numbers of a [restaurant / business] close to you: "Alexa, find the phone number of a [restaurant / business] close to me."

To get their opening and closing hours: "Alexa, find the hours of a [restaurant / business] close to me."

Spelling and Calculations by Alexa

Amazon Alexa can pass for a great dictionary and calculator. Give a try and say, "Alexa, define aquarium," "Alexa, spell the word, magnificent" or "Alexa, convert 100 US dollars to Euros."

Alexa Can Help With Cooking

Recipe skills/services include; Food Network, Recipedia, Good Housekeeping, My Chef, OurGroceries, Instant Pot, Meal Idea, etc.

General invocation format: "Alexa, ask {recipe skill} for a {recipe name}," or "Alexa, ask {skill name} what I can make for [breakfast / lunch / dinner]." To enable any of the skills, simply say, "Alexa, enable {skill name}."

Controlling your TV

You can Alexa to search for movies, change channels, look up content or control playback. This can work with Amazon Fire TV, Fire TV Edition or Fire TV Stick. With Amazon Echo or Echo Dot, you can control Frontier, Fios,

Tivo, Optic Hub, and Dish systems with your voice.

Start by enabling Alexa skill for your device in the Alexa app if necessary. This companion app should come from your satellite or cable provider. You should know how to do this at this time. Next, link up your cable box with your Alexa device via **Settings**. Tap on **TV & Video.**

Select your TV device and **Continue** then choose the Alexa device that's going to be controlling your TV. Note that an Alexa device can only control a TV at one time. Hence, these two should be close together—same room. After selecting your Alexa device, it's time to link it to your Fire TV, scroll down and **Link Devices**.

Think of something you can tell Alexa to do. For example, "Alexa, show a movie with Arnold Schwarzenegger," or "Alexa, show live football matches," etc.

Chapter 10

All You Need to Know About Voice Shopping with Amazon Alexa

Shopping with Alexa using the Amazon Echo devices takes a brand new level. Fortunately and unfortunately, you'll have to be on Amazon Prime to be able to shop using Alexa.

To get started, use the format: "Alexa, buy {product name}," e.g. "Alexa, order Amazon Echo Dot 3rd Generation Black color." From here, Alexa searches through Amazon store and tells you what she found. Follow prompts and buy.

To begin, sign up for Amazon Prime and enable your 1-Click Ordering.

Setting up confirmation code for your shopping

A confirmation code is needed when you've added a product to your cart but not paying for them right away. To set up a code, go to **Menu** , **Settings**, **Alexa Account** on your Alexa app and select Voice Purchasing. Set your 4-digit code. With this code, after adding some items to your cart, Alexa would ask if you are ordering them immediately where your 4-digit code would be required to complete the transaction.

You may not need a confirmation code to complete a purchase if you are searching for and buying the product immediately without necessarily adding it to the cart. For example, you can say, “Alexa, order Amazon Echo Dot from Amazon.” Alexa would now search for the product and return with a reply: “Great, I found Amazon Echo Dot, it’s $49.9, should I place an order for it?” Then you can say, “Go ahead” or “Yes” and your order is placed.

Ordering more than an item of same product or each of different items

If you want to order more than a piece of an item; that would work but if you want to buy different items at the same time or as a single order, that won’t work. So you can say, “Alexa, order 5 pieces of Amazon Echo Input” and not something like, “Alexa, order 2 black Amazon Echo Input and 1 black Amazon Echo Dot 2nd generation.” Voice shopping for different items are done separately or you can add everything to cart and place order with your confirmation code.

More invocation phrases / pattern:

Do you want to re-order essentials from Amazon? "Alexa, buy more deodorant," or "Alexa, re-order deodorant."

You want to search for what to buy? “Alexa, search for {item name}, or “Alexa, find a best-selling {product name}.”

You want to find out cost of a product?
“Alexa, how much is {product name}

You want to track your packages from Amazon? "Alexa, track my order" or "Alexa, where's my stuff?"

You want to order an Alexa device? "Alexa, order an [Alexa device name],"

You want to build your cart?
e.g., "Alexa, add a mouse to my cart."

You want to order Lyft for a ride?
"Alexa, ask Lyft for a ride," where Lyft is a skill by the Lyft company operating cab services. That means you must first of all enable it.

You feel like buying a nice song while listening to it on Amazon Music?
"Alexa, buy this song," or
"Alexa, buy this album."
Or finding a new music to buy?
"Alexa, shop for new music by [artist name]."

Do you want to buy a song / album from a known artist?
"Alexa, buy [song / album] by {artist name}."
You want to know about today's deals?
"Alexa, what are your deals?" or
"Alexa, what deals do you have?"

Buy from Whole Foods Market on Amazon Prime Now

"Alexa, what Whole Foods deals do you have today?"

"Alexa, add {product/item name} to my Whole Foods cart."

Protecting your Voice Purchases

This can help prevent someone else sending a voice command to Alexa to make purchases without your consent. To prevent this, you can create a passcode that Alexa would ask for to confirm request before making purchases. To make it happen, go to Voice Purchases in Settings using the app. You may wish to turn off this function completely.

Chapter 11

News and Information with Alexa

You can hear news from popular broadcasters and news stations including video flashes from Alexa when you set up your Flash Briefings.

To setup your Flash Briefings in the Alexa app, go to **Settings** from the **Menu** then **Flash Briefings** under **Alexa Preferences**. **Toggle** or enable available services listed then tap on **Add Content**. On the ensuing screen, tap on the Search button and begin searching your Flash Briefings with specific skill name. Once found, enable the skill to start using it.

Some popular Flash Briefing skills include; NPR, CBNC, Wall Street Journal, Fox News, Washington Post, BBC News, CNN, Reuters, MTV UK News, etc. Others include Ask Wxbrad (for weather information), Digg (for curated news), Curiosity Daily (for science and technology updates), Marketplace (for news in economics), Daily Tech Headlines (for tech news), Fox Sports (for latest sport news), etc.

Some useful invocation phrases:

To ask for a Flash Briefing, say, "Alexa, what's my Flash Briefing?"

To ask for specific Flash Briefing, say, "Alexa, what are my [News / Sport / Weather etc.] Flash Briefings?" or simply, “Alexa, what’s in the news?”

To navigate stories, say, "Alexa, [next / previous / cancel].”

For video flash briefings, you can say, "Alexa, [pause / stop / resume / continue / next / previous].”

From a particular channel: “Alexa, play my flash briefings from <flash briefing source/skill name>.”

Follow cards that appear on screen for full story if you are using an Echo device with a screen.

Weather and Traffic

In the Alexa app, set your traffic preference to get traffic information within your location. Go to Settings => Alexa Preferences => Traffic. Enter your starting and destination addresses then Save Changes.

To ask for traffic information, say:
“Alexa, how’s traffic?”
“Alexa, how is the traffic right now?”
“Alexa, what is my commute?”
For information on weather in your location, you can say, "Alexa, what's the weather?" or "Alexa, is it going to rain today?" "Alexa, how is the weather this weekend? “Alexa, tell me about the weather in London” or Álexa, tell me about tomorrow’s weather.”

How to Translate Languages using Alexa

Right now, you can translate between these languages using Alexa: French, Spanish, German, Japanese, Italian, Chinese, Polish, Hindi, Portuguese, Dutch, Korean, Danish, Norwegian, Russian, Swedish, Turkish, Romanian, Danish, Icelandic, and Welsh. To try, “Alexa, say goodbye in French.”

Q&A with Alexa

General questions

“Alexa, what’s the population of New York?”

Calculations

“Alexa, what’s 18 times 5?”

Conversions

"Alexa, how many miles do we have in {#} kilometers?"

Trending News and Pop Culture

Follow the trend and get all the facts with Alexa.
Simply ask:
"Alexa, what's trending?"
"Alexa, tell me some weird stuff"

Holidays

You want to find out when next holiday is? "Alexa, when is next holiday?"

You want to hear a holiday limerick? "Alexa, tell me a holiday limerick."

You want to learn about a holiday? "Alexa, why do we celebrate [holiday name]?"

You want to ask about Santa Claus? "Alexa, how old is Santa Claus?," "Alexa, is Santa Claus real?" or "Alexa, where does Santa Claus live?"

You want to track or know where Santa Claus is? "Alexa, where is Santa?" Or "Alexa, track Santa."

You want to listen to a Christmas carol from Alexa? "Alexa, sing a Christmas carol."

You want to hear some holiday jokes? "Alexa, tell me a snowman joke."

You need holiday movies idea? "Alexa, what's your favorite holiday movie?" or "Alexa, what are the top holiday movies?"

Chapter 12

How to fix common issues with the Amazon Echo Dot

Like any electronic, you may encounter common issues, and you can easily fix them.

Inconsistent / no WiFi connection

(a) The common solution is turning off your Router and Echo device then putting them back on.

(b) If the problem isn't fixed after trying (a) above, try to adjust the position of your Echo Dot away from devices that might be blocking or interfering with signals, e.g., microwaves, baby monitors, etc.

Alexa calling not working

(a) Use a supported/compatible device to install Alexa app or make a call. Use Android 5.0 and later on a compatible device.

(b) Check your connection to the internet as well as your signal quality. Signal quality must be strong.

(c) Turn off your internet connection, wait for 30 seconds or more and put it back on.

(d) You can also restart your Android device.

(e) Pull off the power adapter from the Echo device and plug back after 3 seconds while restarting the internet connection.

(f) Confirm that the contact you are trying to call is listed under **Contacts** in **Communication** in the Alexa app. If not listed, sign out and sign in to the Alexa app via **Settings**. For Fire Tablet, go to Account settings, deregister and register the device again.

Difficulty in connecting Alexa to other smart devices

(a) Check for compatibility of your smart device with your Echo. URL: https://www.amazon.com/b?node=6563140011

(b) Check that the companion skill for your smart device is enabled in the Alexa app then try discovering the device by saying, “Alexa, discover devices.”

(c) Make sure your smart home device is on the same network with your Echo Dot.

Alexa doesn't understand my voice

(a) Take the voice training again under **Settings**, tap on **Voice Training**.

(b) Shift the Echo device away from noisy appliances such as the TV, air conditioning vents, stereo, dishwasher, etc.

Difficulty connecting to a Bluetooth device

(a) Ensure your Bluetooth device has sufficient power i.e. the battery is well charged.

(b) Disconnect/unpair and pair up the devices again. To do this, launch the Alexa app, go to **Settings** and select your Echo device then **Bluetooth** and finally **Clear all paired devices**. To repair them, enable your Bluetooth on devices you want to pair with Alexa and say, "Alexa, pair devices."

Streaming services won't work

(a) Check your internet connection.

(b) Check your signal strength.

(c) Check your firewall.

Alexa skill isn’t working

(a) Disable and enable the skill again then restart your Alexa device.

What next when all possible solutions have failed—Factory reset!

Factory reset! Give it a fresh start. To make this happen, while the Echo device is connected to mains, press down the Action button until the Echo Dot enters setup mode with a spinning orange color light.

Chapter 13

Frequently Asked Questions about Amazon Echo Dot 3rd generation

[1] Does Amazon Echo Dot 3rd generation work for multi-room?
Setup may not work on the Alexa mobile app but can be done using a PC.

[2] Can I use more than an Echo Dot in my house?
Yes. You are free but use a different wake-up word to avoid creating confusion them especially if they are within close range.

[3] What language options are currently available?
We have English, German, French and Japanese, Spanish (Mexican) and Spanish (Spain) currently.

[4] Does the Echo Dot 3rd generation operated using battery?
No.

[5] Can I call the emergency with Echo Dot?
No.

[6] Does the Echo Dot save settings?

Yes. When turning on, it uses the latest settings including volume.

[7] Can Google Home and Echo Dot work in the same house?
Yes.

[8] Can multiple Echos play different music simultaneously?
Yes. However, you may encounter some limitations: not with the Echo devices but your music service. For instance, you may not be able to different music from the same Spotify account, but you can play the same music on multiple Echos present in your house.

[9] In the absence of a WiFi network, can I make of a Hotspot?
Yes.

[10] Does the Echo Dot work with other products apart from those of Amazon?
No.

[11] Can this device work with 220V?
Yes. With 50/60 Hz.

[12] Flashing won't go away on my Echo device. Why?
Green light means a notification is pending to be heard. Say, "Alexa, read my notifications." Blue light means the device is trying to connect to the internet. Orange/red light

means the device isn't connected to the internet.

[13] Does the unit permit multi-users?
Yes. Its voice recognition system works great.

[14] Does monthly fees apply for using the device with Amazon?
No. Your regular Amazon account can do but Amazon Prime offers more with Alexa.

[15] Can I use the same Alexa app to run two Echo devices in different locations?
Yes. Simply connect the devices to the app.

[16] Can I still control my Echo device from the app on my phone when I am away from home?
Yes. You can do that from the Alexa app.

[17] Can I use the Echo Dot to do other things rather than always depending on Amazon?
Yes. You can also connect a tablet or smartphone to it via Bluetooth. After pairing the devices together, you can say something like, "Alexa, connect iPhone" or "Alexa, disconnect iPhone."

[18] Is the Echo Dot 3rd generation work with an adapter that is USB?
No.

[19] Can I connect wired headphones to the Echo Dot?
Yes. There's a provision for it.

[20] Do you need more products to have the Echo Dot working for you?
No. The Alexa app will do.

****

Claim your free eBook

Send an email to:

siggny1@gmail.com

Thank you for your purchase.

38443500R00066

Made in the USA
Lexington, KY
08 May 2019